North Carolina

by Patricia K. Kummer,
the Capstone Press Geography Department

Content Consultant:
Susan Temple
Elementary Social Studies Consultant
North Carolina Department of Public Instruction

CAPSTONE PRESS
MANKATO, MINNESOTA

C A P S T O N E P R E S S

818 North Willow Street • Mankato, MN 56001

http://www.capstone-press.com

Printed in the United States of America.

Library of Congress Cataloging-in-Publication Data
Kummer, Patricia K.
　　North Carolina/by Patricia K. Kummer (Capstone Press Geography Department).
　　　p. cm.--(One nation)
　　Includes bibliographical references and index.
　　Summary: An overview of the history, geography, people, and living conditions of the state of North Carolina.
　　ISBN 1-56065-530-5
　　1. North Carolina--Juvenile literature. [1. North Carolina]
　　I. Capstone Press. Geography Dept. II. Title. III. Series.
F254.3.K86 1998
975.6--dc21

97-7069
CIP
AC

Photo credits
The Bettmann Archive, 25, 29
Capstone Press, 4 (left)
Dare County Tourist Bureau, 6
William B. Folsom, cover
High Point Convention and Visitors Bureau, 26
North Carolina Travel and Tourism, 5 (left), 8, 10, 12, 16, 21, 30, 32, 34
Root Resources/Anthony Mercieca, 4 (right)
James P. Rowan, 18
Unicorn Stock/Gurmankin and Morina, 5 (right); Andre Jenny, 22

CY5/98

Table of Contents

Fast Facts about North Carolina

State Flag

Location: Along the Atlantic Ocean in the southeastern United States

Size: 53,821 square miles (139,935 square kilometers)

Population: 7,195,138 (1995 United States Census Bureau figures)

Capital: Raleigh

Date admitted to the Union: November 21, 1789; the 12th state

Cardinal

Flowering dogwood

Largest cities:
Charlotte,
Raleigh,
Greensboro,
Winston-Salem,
Durham,
Fayetteville,
High Point,
Asheville,
Wilmington,
Gastonia

Nickname: The Tar Heel State
State bird: Cardinal
State flower:
Flowering
dogwood
State tree:
Longleaf pine
State song: "The
Old North State"
by William
Gaston and Mrs.
E. E. Randolph

Longleaf pine

Chapter 1

The Lost Colony

North Carolina's Roanoke Island is the setting of a great mystery. In July 1587, about 120 English colonists settled there. They were led by Sir Walter Raleigh. His colony was England's first in the newly discovered America. A colony is a group of people who settle in a distant land but remain governed by their native country.

In 1590, a supply ship came to the island. No one came to meet the ship. The colony had completely disappeared.

The crew of the ship found a word carved into a tree. It said "Croatoan." The crew started

The supply ship could not find Sir Walter Raleigh's colony in 1590.

The Blue Ridge Parkway is a scenic highway that runs through western North Carolina.

to look for the lost colony. But bad weather forced the crew back to England. The colonists were never found.

Some historians think the colonists ran out of food. They believe the colonists may have moved to present-day Hatteras Island or to the Chesapeake Bay area. Friendly Croatoan Indians lived there.

Some Indians, such as the Lumbee, say they have come from the Croatoan Indians. They claim their families included the lost colonists.

Some of them have blue eyes and English last names.

Visiting North Carolina

People still come to North Carolina to learn about the lost colony. They visit the Fort Raleigh National Historic Site. An outdoor play about the colonists is presented there every summer.

North Carolina offers other places to visit, too. Millions of people enjoy the Blue Ridge Parkway. This scenic roadway runs through western North Carolina and Virginia.

More than 8 million people visit Great Smoky Mountains National Park each year. It lies in North Carolina and Tennessee. This is the country's most-visited national park.

The Tar Heel State

North Carolina's nickname is the Tar Heel State. In the 1700s, North Carolina began a naval stores business. Naval stores are goods including turpentine and tar.

Tar was used to repair ships. The tar stuck to workers' hands and feet. The workers were called Tar Heels.

Chapter 2
The Land

Northern Carolina is the fourth largest southern state. Four other southern states are its neighbors. Virginia lies to the north. Tennessee is to the west. Georgia and South Carolina lie to the south.

The Atlantic Ocean forms North Carolina's eastern border. North Carolina's lowest point is along the Atlantic coast. This point is sea level.

The Outer Banks
North Carolina's tidal shoreline is 3,375 miles (5,400 kilometers) long. Tidal shoreline is any land that is touched by ocean waters. Part of this shoreline is the Outer Banks. This is a long

Cape Hatteras is one of the capes on the Outer Banks. Cape Hatteras lighthouse started warning ships in 1870.

Mount Mitchell is North Carolina's highest point. It is in the Black Mountain range.

stretch of sandbars and islands. Ocracoke and Hatteras are two large islands.

Three capes are also located on the Outer Banks. A cape is part of a coastline that sticks out into the sea. The three capes are Cape Fear, Cape Lookout, and Cape Hatteras. Cape Hatteras is known as the Graveyard of the Atlantic. The cape's sand shifts. This shifting sand has caused many ships to run aground.

The Atlantic Coastal Plain

Almost half of North Carolina is part of the Coastal Plain. This land is low. Wetlands lie near the coast. Part of the Great Dismal Swamp is in North Carolina. The rest is in Virginia. Cypress trees grow in the swamps.

The western part of the Coastal Plain has the state's richest farmland. Tobacco grows well there.

The Piedmont

The Piedmont covers the middle of North Carolina. Piedmont means "at the foot of a mountain." The Appalachian Mountains rise at the Piedmont's western edge.

Land on the Piedmont is hilly. The state's six largest cities were built there.

The Appalachian Mountains

Several Appalachian mountain ranges are in North Carolina. They include the Blue Ridge and Great Smoky mountains.

North Carolina's highest point is Mount Mitchell. This is in the Black Mountains. It is also the highest point east of the Mississippi river. Mount Mitchell rises 6,684 feet (2,005 meters) above sea level.

Two national forests cover North Carolina's mountains. They are the Pisgah National Forest and the Nantahala National Forest.

Lakes and Rivers

North Carolina's natural lakes are in the east. Lake Mattamuskeet is the largest one. The Piedmont has many lakes made by humans. Lake Norman is the biggest one. A dam on the Catawba River formed it.

The state's eastern rivers flow into the Atlantic Ocean. They include the Roanoke, Pamlico, Neuse, and Cape Fear. The Pee Dee and the Yadkin are rivers in the Piedmont.

Climate

Most of North Carolina has hot, wet summers. The winters are mild to cold. The weather is cooler in the mountains.

Strong windstorms called hurricanes sometimes hit the coast and cause damage. More hurricanes pass Cape Hatteras than any other point in the world.

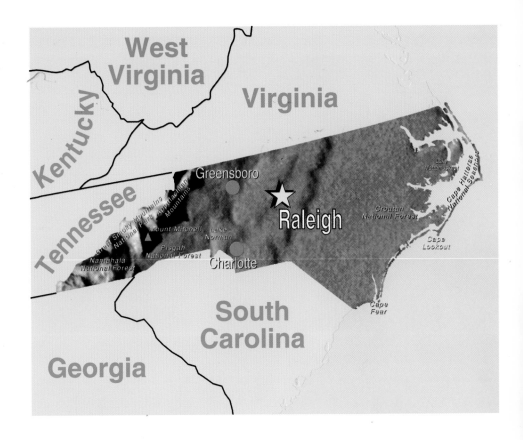

Wildlife

Wild ponies run free along the Outer Banks. Dolphins and marlins swim off the coast. Flocks of ducks and geese spend the winter in coastal marshes. Deer roam North Carolina's woods. Black bears live in the mountains.

Chapter 3
The People

North Carolina has the nation's 10th largest population. The state has gained many people in recent years.

Jobs draw many new people to the state. They settle in cities on the Piedmont. Others retire in North Carolina. Many retired people live in the Asheville area.

Native Americans

More than 80,000 Native Americans live in North Carolina. This is the nation's seventh largest number of Native Americans.

The Cherokee are North Carolina's largest Native American group. In the 1830s, European

The Cherokee are North Carolina's largest Native American group.

The Oconaluftee Indian Village is a restored village from the 1700s.

settlers tried to force the Cherokee to leave North Carolina's land. The Cherokee refused. Today, many Cherokee live on the Eastern Cherokee Reservation. This reservation is in the Great Smoky Mountains.

The Oconaluftee Indian Village is on the reservation. This is a restored village from the 1700s. During the summer, the Cherokee present a play called *Unto These Hills*. It tells of the forced removal of the Cherokee.

European Ethnic Groups

Almost 76 percent of North Carolinians are white. Many of them are the families of North Carolina's first European settlers.

The first permanent European settlers had English backgrounds. They came from Virginia in the 1650s. These people settled along Albemarle Sound.

People from Scotland settled along the Cape Fear River. They founded Fayetteville in 1739. Each July, North Carolina's Scots host the Highland Games at Grandfather Mountain.

In the 1750s, Germans and Scotch-Irish came from Pennsylvania. They settled on the Piedmont. Today, North Carolina has the nation's largest number of Scotch-Irish.

African Americans

In the 1650s, Africans arrived in North Carolina as slaves. By 1860, slaves made up one-third of North Carolina's population. Most of them worked on tobacco plantations. A plantation is a large farm.

Many free African Americans also lived in North Carolina. Some of them had bought their freedom.

After the Civil War (1861-1865), all the slaves were freed. In the 1890s, North Carolina passed laws making it hard for African Americans to vote. African Americans were kept separate from whites. They had a hard time finding work.

In the 1900s, thousands of African Americans left North Carolina. They moved north.

Today, 22 percent of North Carolinians are African American. Many African Americans are moving back to North Carolina. They have won equal rights.

Other Ethnic Groups

About 50,000 Asian Americans live in North Carolina. Most of them have Indian or Chinese backgrounds. Fayetteville has a large Korean population. Many people from Thailand live in Wayne County.

Many African Americans worked as slaves on tobacco plantations in the 1860s.

North Carolina has about 69,000 Hispanic Americans. Most of these Spanish-speaking people came from Mexico. Chapel Hill's Hispanics host a festival each September.

Chapter 4

North Carolina History

People first lived in North Carolina about 12,000 years ago. By the 1500s, more than 35,000 Native Americans lived in the area. The Cherokee, Tuscarora, and Croatoan were the major groups.

Europeans arrived in the 1500s. French and Spanish explorers sailed near Cape Fear. In 1587, English colonists settled on Roanoke Island. That colony lasted only a few years.

A Permanent English Colony

In the 1600s, the English claimed parts of North America. They settled 13 colonies along the Atlantic Ocean.

In 1587, English colonists settled on Roanoke Island.

North Carolina's first permanent settlers arrived in the 1650s. They were English farmers from Virginia. Later, more Europeans came. They settled on Native American land.

Indian Wars and Pirates

The English colonists and Native Americans fought over land. The Tuscarora destroyed many English settlements. The colonists defeated the Tuscarora in the Tuscarora War (1711-1713). Most of the Tuscarora left North Carolina.

During those same years, pirates attacked ships along the coast. A pirate is a person who attacks and steals from ships at sea. In 1718, the pirate Blackbeard was killed near Ocracoke Island. After that, most pirate attacks ended.

In 1760, North Carolinians defeated the Cherokee. This victory opened western North Carolina to settlers.

The Revolutionary War and the Constitution

The colonists started the Revolutionary War in 1775. They wanted freedom from England's control. North Carolina was the first colony to call for independence from England. North

The pirate Blackbeard was killed near North Carolina's Ocracoke Island in 1718.

Carolinians helped win the war. In 1783, the colonies became the United States of America.

The country's new leaders wrote a constitution. North Carolina approved the United States Constitution in 1789. It became the 12th state.

At first, North Carolina grew slowly. Most western settlers had small farms. Many eastern landowners had plantations. Tobacco and cotton were important crops.

The Civil War and Reconstruction

Slavery divided the United States. Southerners feared the U.S. government would outlaw slavery. They wanted slaves to work on their plantations.

Many Southern states seceded from the Union of states. To secede means to formally withdraw. They formed the Confederate States of America. This led to the Civil War (1861-1865). After the war started, North Carolina seceded. It was the last state to do so.

When the war ended, the state lay in ruins. All the slaves were freed. North Carolina wrote a new state constitution. African-American men gained voting rights. In 1868, North Carolina was allowed to rejoin the Union.

Farming and New Industries

After the Civil War, the state's plantations were broken up. Poor whites and African Americans became tenant farmers. A tenant farmer is one who rents land to farm and pays the rent in crops. Tenant farmers had a hard time making a living.

Factories went up on the Piedmont. High Point became a center for making wooden furniture and its coverings. Durham became

After the Civil War, High Point became a center for making wooden furniture and its coverings.

famous for making cigarettes. Textile mills were built along fast-running rivers.

World Wars and Depression

In 1917, the United States entered World War I (1914-1918). Thousands of troops trained at Fort Bragg army base. Wilmington's shipyards built 30 ships for the navy.

The entire country suffered during the Great Depression (1929-1939). Farmers lost their land. Thousands of workers lost their jobs. The United States and North Carolina set up job programs. North Carolinians built new roads and cleaned up state parks.

In 1941, the United States entered World War II (1939-1945). Marine bases opened at Camp Lejeune and Cherry Point. The state's textile mills provided cloth for uniforms.

New Rights for African Americans

Since the 1890s, the southern states had kept whites and African Americans separated. In February 1960, African Americans in Greensboro worked to be treated as equals. They held the nation's first sit-in. A sit-in is an event where

African Americans held a sit-in at a lunch counter that served only white people.

people sit in a specific place to protest something. This took place at a lunch counter that served only white people. By July, the city's lunch counters were no longer separated by race. Most schools were no longer separated by the 1970s.

Today, North Carolina continues to improve itself. North Carolinians are making their schools better. The government has invited new businesses to the state.

Chapter 5

North Carolina Business

Manufacturing is North Carolina's largest business. Taken together, however, service industries lead the state's businesses. Tourism, research, and government are important service industries.

Manufacturing

North Carolina leads the nation in making tobacco products, wooden furniture, and textiles. Textiles are yarns, fibers, and cloth. Greensboro has the world's largest denim mill. Denim is used to make jeans. High Point is called the Furniture Capital of America. North Carolinians also make chemicals, paper, computers, and telephones.

The Biltmore Estate is one of the tourist attractions that makes tourism an important service industry.

Research Triangle Park is a major research center. It is located between Chapel Hill, Durham, and Raleigh.

Service Industries

Tourism is a big service industry. Each year, tourists spend about $8 billion in North Carolina. Restaurants, hotels, and motels receive most of this money.

Government services include public education and military training. North Carolina has a large public university system. Camp Lejeune is a major marine base. Fort Bragg is a large army base.

Research Triangle Park is a major research center. It lies between Chapel Hill, Durham, and Raleigh. Companies from all over the country do research there. Research is a study to learn new facts or solve a problem.

Agriculture

Farming is important in North Carolina. North Carolina leads the states in growing tobacco. Corn, soybeans, peanuts, and sweet potatoes are other important crops. They grow on the Coastal Plain. Apples and peaches grow on the Piedmont.

Broiler chickens and hogs are the state's leading livestock products. North Carolina is a leading turkey producer, too.

Mining and Fishing

North Carolina has more than 300 kinds of minerals. Limestone is North Carolina's leading mineral product. The state is a major producer of feldspar and mica. Feldspar is a mineral used to make glass. Mica is used in electronics.

Shrimp, blue crabs, and clams are valuable to the fishing industry. Aquaculture also takes place in North Carolina. Aquaculture is raising fish or crops in water. Catfish and crayfish are raised on special fish farms.

Chapter 6

Seeing the Sights

Each year, millions of people visit North Carolina. Many enjoy the state's beaches and mountains. Others learn about North Carolina's history.

The Outer Banks

Kill Devil Hills is on Bodie Island. Orville and Wilbur Wright made the first powered airplane flight there in 1903. Strong winds helped them take off. The sandy beaches provided soft landings. The Wright brothers built the plane at their headquarters in Kitty Hawk.

Roanoke Island is southwest of Kill Devil Hills. Fort Raleigh National Historic Site stands there. Visitors learn about the Lost Colony. The

Many visitors enjoy seeing the sleeping face of an old man on Grandfather Mountain.

North Carolina Aquarium is also on the island. It has a popular shark exhibit.

Hatteras Island is south of Roanoke. Cape Hatteras Lighthouse stands at the cape's point. Since 1870, it has warned ships of danger. Visitors can climb its 268 steps to the top.

Hatteras National Seashore covers Brodie, Hatteras, and Ocracoke islands. Snow geese and Canada geese nest there. People enjoy its beaches. They swim, fish, and camp.

The Coastal Plain

The northeastern Coastal Plain is called the Cradle of North Carolina. The state's first settlements were located there. Elizabeth City has the Museum of the Albemarle. Visitors go there to learn about the state's early history.

New Bern is on the Neuse River in the middle of the coast. This town was North Carolina's colonial capital in the 1770s. Tryon Palace was the first state capitol building. The building and its garden have been restored.

Croatoan National Forest is south of New Bern. Alligators swim in its lakes. People can swim in the Neuse River. Hunters can track deer and bears.

Wilmington is at the state's southern tip. This city is North Carolina's main port. The USS *North Carolina* is docked there. This battleship was used during World War II.

The Piedmont

North Carolina's largest cities are on the Piedmont. Raleigh is in the east-central part of the state. It has been the state capital since 1792. The North Carolina Museum of Natural History is in Raleigh. Visitors can see a whale's skeleton and a live python. North Carolina State University is in Raleigh, too.

Durham is northwest of Raleigh. The North Carolina Mutual Life Insurance Company has headquarters there. This company was founded by African Americans in 1898. Duke University is also in Durham.

Chapel Hill is west of Durham. It is home to the University of North Carolina. Michael Jordan played basketball there.

Burlington is northwest of Chapel Hill. Shoppers can visit more than 150 outlet stores there. Level Cross is southwest of Burlington. The Richard Petty Museum is there. It displays the famous driver's racing cars.

Winston-Salem is west of Burlington. Old Salem is there. This is a restored Moravian town. Costumed guides cook using Moravian recipes. The Moravians founded Salem in 1766.

Charlotte is south of Winston-Salem. This is North Carolina's largest city. Discovery Place is a hands-on science museum in Charlotte. The museum has an aquarium, a rain forest, and a planetarium. Charlotte is also home to the NBA Hornets and the Carolina Panthers football team.

Western North Carolina

Mountains and forests cover western North Carolina. Many waterfalls tumble down to southwestern rivers. Whitewater Falls is in the Nantahala National Forest. It drops 411 feet (123 meters) into the White River.

Asheville is east of Nantahala National Forest. This city is in the Blue Ridge Mountains. It is North Carolina's headquarters for Great Smoky Mountains National Park. The Blue Ridge Parkway winds around and through Asheville.

The Folk Art Center is in Asheville. It keeps Appalachian arts and crafts alive. Visitors can buy quilts, baskets, and pottery made by North Carolina crafters.

Asheville is also home to the Biltmore Estate. Visitors can tour this 250-room mansion and its gardens.

Grandfather Mountain is northeast along the Blue Ridge Parkway. This mountain looks like the sleeping face of an old man. Brave visitors can cross the mountain's Mile-High Swinging Bridge.

North Carolina Time Line

10,000 B.C.—People are living in North Carolina.

A.D. 1500—About 35,000 Native Americans are living in North Carolina, including Cherokee, Croatoan, Catawba, and Tuscarora.

1584—English explorers sail along the coast.

1590—The colony on Roanoke has disappeared.

1650s—The first English colonists arrive in the Albemarle Sound area.

1711-1713—The Tuscarora War ends with the defeat of the Native Americans.

1718—Blackbeard is killed near Ocracoke Island.

1729—North Carolina becomes an English colony.

1775-1783—North Carolina helps the 13 colonies win their independence from England.

1781—U.S. troops lose the Battle of Guilford Courthouse but cause heavy English losses.

1789—North Carolina becomes the 12th state.

1792—Raleigh is named the state capital.

1795—The University of North Carolina opens and becomes the nation's first state university.

1845—North Carolina native James Polk becomes the 11th president of the United States.

1861—The Civil War begins; North Carolina secedes from the Union and joins the Confederacy.

1865—The Civil War ends; North Carolina native Andrew Johnson becomes the 17th president of the United States.

1868—North Carolina is readmitted to the Union.

1901—Governor Charles Aycock begins a program to improve North Carolina's schools.

1903—The Wright brothers make the first successful airplane flight at Kitty Hawk.

1915—North Carolina begins to build roads.

1926—Great Smoky Mountains National Park is established in North Carolina and Tennessee.

1936—The Intracoastal Waterway is complete.

1942—Camp Lejeune opens.

1954—Hurricane Hazel kills 19 people and causes $136 million in damage.

1959—Research Triangle Park opens.

1960—The first sit-in is held by four African Americans after they are refused service at Woolworth's lunch counter in Greensboro.

1989—Hurricane Hugo kills at least two people and causes $1 billion in damage.

1991—A fire in a Hamlet chicken-processing plant kills 25 people.

1995—The Panthers play their first football season.

1995-1996—African-American churches are burned.

1996—Jesse Helms wins a fifth U.S. Senate term.

Famous North Carolinians

David Brinkley (1920-) Television journalist and newscaster who hosted *This Week with David Brinkley* (1981-1996); born in Wilmington.

Betsy Byars (1928-) Newbery Medal-winner for *The Summer of the Swans*; born in Charlotte.

Virginia Dare (1587- ?) The first English child born in America; she and her family were part of the Lost Colony; born on Roanoke Island.

Elizabeth Hanford Dole (1936-) Secretary of Transportation (1983-1987); Secretary of Labor (1989-1990); president of the American Red Cross (1990-present); helped her husband Bob campaign for the presidency (1996); born in Salisbury.

Billy Graham (1918-) Evangelist who has preached at big rallies around the world; born in Charlotte.

Roberta Flack (1940-) Grammy Award-winning singer whose hits include "Killing Me Softly with His Song"; born in Black Mountain.

Andy Griffith (1926-) Television actor in *The Andy Griffith Show* and *Matlock*; born in Mount Airy.

Pleasant Hanes (1845-1925) Founder of the Hanes Corporation; born in Winston-Salem.

Jim "Catfish" Hunter (1946-) Hall of Fame pitcher for World Series champion Oakland Athletics and New York Yankees; born in Hertford.

Michael Jordan (1963-) University of North Carolina NCAA basketball champ (1982); led the Chicago Bulls to the NBA championship four times (1991, 1992, 1993, 1996).

Charles Kuralt (1934-) Television newscaster known for his show *On the Road*; born in Wilmington.

Herman Lay (1909-1982) Potato chip salesman who bought the company that became Frito-Lay, Inc.; born in Charlotte.

Sugar Ray Leonard (1956-) Boxing champion and Olympic gold medalist (1976); born in Wilmington.

Dolley Payne Madison (1768-1849) Wife of President James Madison; saved a famous portrait of George Washington during the War of 1812; born in Guilford County.

Edward R. Murrow (1908-1965) Radio journalist during World War II; born in Greensboro.

William Sydney Porter (1862-1910) Writer who used the pen name of O. Henry; born in Greensboro.

Hiram Revels (1822-1901) First African American elected to the U.S. Senate; born in Fayetteville.

Words to Know

aquaculture—the work of raising fish or crops in water

cape—part of a coastline that sticks out into the sea

colony—a group of people who settle in a distant land but remain governed by their native country

hurricane—a strong windstorm that forms over an ocean and causes great damage when it hits land

naval stores—goods such as tar and turpentine

research—a study to learn new facts or solve a problem

pirate—a person who attacks and steals from ships at sea

secede—to formally withdraw

sit-in—an event where people sit in a specific place to protest something

tenant farmer—one who rents land to farm and pays the rent in crops

tidal shoreline—any land that is touched by ocean waters

To Learn More

Aylesworth, Thomas G. and Virginia L. Aylesworth. *Lower Atlantic*. New York: Chelsea House, 1991.

Fradin, Dennis B. *North Carolina*. Sea to Shining Sea. Chicago: Children's Press, 1992.

Fradin, Dennis B. *The North Carolina Colony*. Chicago: Children's Press, 1991.

Kuralt, Charles and Loonis McGlohon. *North Carolina Is My Home*. Chester, Conn.: The Globe Pequot Press, 1986.

Schulz, Andrea. *North Carolina*. Minneapolis: Lerner Publications, 1993.

Useful Addresses

Biltmore Homespun Shops and Museum
111 Grovewood Road
Asheville, NC 28804

Cape Hatteras National Seashore
Route 1, Box 675
Manteo, NC 27954

Discovery Place
301 North Tryon Place
Charlotte, NC 28202

Eastern Band of Cherokee Indians
P.O. Box 455
Cherokee, NC 28719

Penland School of Crafts
P.O. Box 37
Penland, NC 28765

Tryon Palace
610 Pollack Street
New Bern, NC 28560

Internet Sites

City.Net North Carolina
http://www.city.net/countries/united_states/
north_carolina

Travel.org—North Carolina
http://travel.org/n-carol.html

North Carolina Information
http://www.sips.state.nc.us

Roanoke Island
http://www.outer-banks.nc.us/tourism/roanoke.htm

Index